In Passion's
Unmade Bed

4 In Passion's Unmade Bed

In Passion's
Unmade Bed

Published by Barrington Teasdale Illinois 1995

Library of Congress Cataloging in Publication Data

Shantell, Juliet
    In passion's unmade bed/ Juliet Shantell
        p.   cm.
     ISBN 0-9641562-2-9
     1. Love poetry, American. 1. Title
    PS3569.H337515   1995
    811' .54--dc20
Library of Congress Catalog Card Number 94-47327

PRINTED IN THE UNITED STATES OF AMERICA

Thank You

My Knight In Shining Armor: for giving me your heart so many years ago

"Baby Doll": for being my one and only masterpiece (of all the things I'll ever create in my lifetime)

My Parents: for being foremost and always my biggest fans

Marijo: for your smiles and creativity

Jennifer: for graciously offering the photograph that appears on the cover

My Lord And Savior: for talents and gifts bestowed upon me

A NOTE FROM THE AUTHOR

These are mere lines on pages
It is a lesson in feeling
One of the hearts is yours

Love
is a hands-on
experience

Each of you who read these lines
will be taken to a familiar
place

Poetry is always
a
two-way street

We can't walk down it
without bringing someone back
and these are mere lines on pages

Table of Contents

In Passion's Unmade Bed

INDELIBLE FEELINGS

Love's quiet rapture like witchcraft
can cast a spell or tempt fate,
in watercolors and lipstick traces
it lingers.

Some lost lovers still echo within
and will not let our hearts run free,
but those like never before
stay soul-mates in heart
and in soul–

They are the example
for all lovers yet to come.
So when ecstasy stirs
in some wintry cabin
or along some moonlit beach—
each will be the yard stick.

In a lover's embrace some night,
passion will tempt your soul
and find that love you thought
was tucked away,
that had no key to enter into it,
A prom rose pressed between pages
in a yearbook holds the love
of treasured moments.

WILL YOU STILL FIND MAGIC?

Will you
still find magic underneath
the covers with me when the years
have turned my hair to silver?
Will you bestow your passion
upon my fragile frame?
Will you still desire me long
after time has made senior
citizens of us...Or when
other men still wink at me
with lustful eyes?...Will
you desire my body when
I no longer move with a
ballerina's grace or when
my disposition does not
always keep you
in the mood?

Will you flood me with an avalanche of
passion as you do tonight when my bedroom
eyes grow dim with age?

Will I be able to reach out for you and still
find you there when my twilight years grow
few?...

Will you wake me with your love in the
morning when our love making no longer
fits into the national average?

Will you still be here when my night cream
can no longer conceal my character lines?...
And will you still desire me the night that
I want to sleep in a seperate bed?

AND STILL YOU LOVE

Your love is your loneliness unhidden.
And the very same heart from which your
Tenderness flows was oftentimes made
Complete by your solitude.
So how else can this be?

The greater that love engraves into your heart,
The more happiness you can hold.
Is not the moonlit sky you dance under now,
The very same sky that was cloudy and gray?

When you are in love,
See deep into your soul and you shall understand
It is only that which has given you loneliness
That is giving you love.

When you are lonely see again into your soul,
And you shall understand that in your solitude
You are lovesick for that which
Has been your happiness.

DIMENSIONS IN OUR UNITY

We love each other,
But create not a warranty of love:
We are rather a bright horizon
Between the eternity of our hearts.
Making complete each others' dream but we slumber
Not from one dream.

Finding solace on the rock of each others' love
But standing not on the same plateau.
Together we are happy,
But we each love our solitude.
Just as the stars of night stand apart,
They still are attached to the heavens.

We give our souls,
But not into each other's possession.
For only the seasons of Freedom
Can embody our souls.
And we touch yet
We do not intertwine.

INTERPRETATION OF LOVE

There is a place where love burns as bright as candles
and a place where the unwillingness to love
is worst than any divorce.

There is a caress of two bodies
that can send reason out the door.

There is a look from a pair of passing eyes
that is as penetrating as electricity.

There is a moment of passion that baffles
all philosophy books.

Caresses, looks, moments of passion—
from these love makes war and peace.

There is a coffee mug love drinks from.

There is a time love gives and the length
of it is never measured till later.

There are languages of love in many tongues
and we can decipher all as:

There is a place where love burns as bright as
candles and a place where the unwillingness to
love is worst than divorce.

FIRST ROMANCE

You had carte blanche
touch by touch
....Love is a Saturday night movie
played back in slow motion

You gave me my first Valentine
to let my heart run free
with no brakes
...I now reclaim this passion
and pour it upon you
like warm syrup
over waffles

My soul was in the
rebirth stage

This probably will not etch us
in stone...or have you somewhere calling
my name in the middle of the
night...But a great burden
has been lifted from my heart and

I can dance in the pouring
rain and not mind getting wet

Layer by layer
...you unraveled me
like a ball of yarn
Love is a Saturday night
movie played back in slow
motion...And

Carte blanche is the
passion reclaimed
again and again

LOVERS

Lovers are a rare breed
not every couple can be

It's not just candlelight and wine
It's more than bedroom eyes and satin sheets
Loving someone
is an art
...It can't be taken
or rushed or
lost

Real lovers give without
ulterior motives and
(I feel) true love can
transcend all pain

Commitment is no stranger
to love...Bonds bred in the
heart are the strongest kind

Silver and gold wedding
anniversaries are not
by chance

Lovers are a rare breed
not every couple can be

ODE TO A FAIR YOUNG MAIDEN

She faced the first time
Her rose-colored glasses came off
And when her paper doll world
Was about to be invaded
Upon her fragile frame bore
The passion of all his love
And a tingle that only she feels
Still dances in midnight dreams
At the center of her soul.

Be ever so cautious in how you take her heart
For she will be alert
After all, loving is her only liberation.
And when you step into her mind
You will be astonished at
The way you can see forever
In her ever-calling eyes.

HEARTS

Hearts that bare no scars
have no secrets to tell
for a secret told
is a secret no more.

Hearts that stay homeless
become prisoners of their own
freedom but a prisoner held
captive by love is a prisoner
no more.

Hearts that never dance for
love end up as dance-away
lovers but lovers that dance into
the flame of love are dance-away
lovers no more.

A TOAST TO YOU

I love you with all
my souls to come,
your love engulfs me-
the more my passions flow
the more I desire.

I am glad you
happened to me-
knowing the strength
of your love-
only you can sing
my heart song.

MEMO TO MY HEART

The timeless glamour of forever sends
chills up my spine and down again.

One smile makes another.
Recent love makes me nostalgic for
love long ago.

Passion is the same each time:
seen in different faces,
felt through different hearts,
it is still love answering love.

I begin this day
in passion's unmade bed.

KEEP MY SECRETS

Keep my secrets
In your heart's treasure chest:
Hide my passions deep within.
Only you can know
Why my heart sighs,
This tree of love
Growing in your sun.

PLACES

There is a place inside of you
that belongs only to me
where dreams have been
where your love pours
to over flowing.

There is a place inside of me
that still loves you deep in the
back of my heart where
your love haunts my mind
like the chorus of an old
familiar song.

CHECKING OUT TIME IS 2 P.M.

I thought at times
one-night stands were lovers
in motel rooms
of my own selection
then not lovers anymore.

I guess they call it
            loneliness
because everybody needs
or wants comfort.
I did.
Some nights.
The magic of seduction
    and the thrill of passion.
The glimpse of forever.

In time I'm sure I will return.
Those one-night stands
will find me an easy prey,
defenseless except for your initials
        tattooed on my left thigh.

MY ABANDON HEART

I know that love is not so mercurial
that it will not find its' way to my heart
leaving me to fend for myself one day at such
an inopportune moment in my life.
So I wait.

I have often thought of past lovers
            in private.

I will take love's path least traveled and
hope one day to find a special someone that
will put a nightcap on each day and lay my
heart down on satin sheets each night.

ONE WHITE ROSE

He gave her a rose
white
pure
and sweeter than any flower known to man
to place on her pillow.

summer wind...
balmy breeze blows through her
and her hair falls gently over one eye:
balmy breeze and expensive perfume
pure and sensuous
ripple through the denim
of her high school jacket

She is a white rose
pure as snow, innocent
and sweeter than any flower
known to man,
in a moonlit night
a satin dream of all young males.

THE OUTER REACHES OF MY HEART

Our souls have known each other for eternity
Although we've only been together for a short time.
I constantly find a part of you always near,
Here at the outer reaches of my heart.

On this path we are traveling
It brings us closer still,
I know I will always
Have love so unhurried
Here at the outer reaches of my heart.

So take my hand
And we will find the Holy Grail,
I will shout our love from rooftops
Here at the outer reaches of my heart.

I know that time will seal our fate,
Our love will be written in the stars
And when it finally is,
I will take comfort
Here at the outer reaches of my heart.

LOVE'S TRAGIC CONTRADICTION

There is an old lover in my memory-
Enraptured in my eternal soul
Living in a room deep inside me
That you nor any other lover has ever entered.

I am not exempt from you.
Why is it that the people
We love the most
Always love someone else?

Your love is made of something strong.
You always give much more than I need,
And I always end up taking much more than I give.

Some hearts never find love in a lifetime.
They are destined to search forever.
Others find love and not knowing it is
Love that they have found,
Toss it aside for cheaper thrills.

THE ONE THAT GOT AWAY

Looking through an old diary
I can see your face...
from my memory
comes your voice
can a lover hear a song of
yesterday and still remember?
all of the suitors and all those
romantic places
all the times
I let my heart run free
and I am untouched still
I feel I will play solitaire
from time to time
all of my life
sealing my fate
with lost and found lovers
hoping you might call
hearing our favorite song
still remembering hearts
I have broken
I catch myself missing you

INTO THE ABYSS

If I had known how love is
I would have locked the door
of my heart's room.
I would have stayed far away,
But you are already here.

Yet here still...
Even as ecstasy floods the bed.
Keep pouring the love,
I long to lose my soul.

SWEPT AWAY

I fell in love the first time your eyes met mine.
And I knew I would never make it out again.
Like a tide that comes over me,
The undercurrent too strong.
Each glance burned at my heart.
The heat of animal magnetism.
I sent out an s.o.s. for my emotional emergency.
Yet I knew you wanted to go deeper
Into my soul than anyone has ever been.
After all, we both knew it was going to happen
The only thing was when.

SHIPS THAT PASS IN THE NIGHT

Blue blue forget-me-not

turquoise sounds of a sexy ballad
down a hall
soft and mellow with sunset

She
listens to the music
in the heat of this Indian summer night

He is at the foot
of the bed,
steel-gray eyes
and wavy hair,
blowing smoke rings
in the dark

The velvet maroon drapes
the satin ruby-red sheets
of love's after-glow
kindles forever
these two passing strangers

THE DELICATE TAPESTRY OF LOVE

You have merit enough
to fill an eternity,
maybe more,
within these close
quiet moments.

Two lovers loving,
bestowing gifts of the heart
upon one another.
Candlelight and wine.
Red roses and satin sheets.

The nooks and crannies
of your heart
see inside my soul.
Your love now
even more apparent
fills the night
as if to music and dance.

IT CAN BE FOREVER

We have earned the honor
For the stars to write
Our name across the heavens.

I am of the belief
That the Gods of passion
Bestow membership upon
Its' truest lovers.

After all,
Our hearts tell time only
By eternity's clock,
And by love's
Eternal hourglass.

DAY DREAMING

A part of you is always here.
From my pillow comes the
scent of your after-shave.
Can a lover hear a song
on the radio and
be swept away?

Bedroom eyes and satin sheets.
All the times when you take
my hand and we press love
into the chambers of our hearts.
It is at these times
I feel a special coming together.

Waiting for you to come home.
Still remembering last night.
I love you now,
I will love you even far from now.

CUTS TO THE QUICK

You are fragile and susceptible
like a candle in the wind,
your heart still bears the scar

You bleed

a curious wanderlust beckons your soul
like a traveler who has overstayed
his welcome

You are leaving
I am the last to forget
the last to let go
and memories aren't replacable

Yet you came closer than the rest
close enough to touch
my broken heart

After all, we were
a rare and beautiful moment
that came once and
would never come again

INESCAPABLE MEMORIES

I find it easy to understand
past lovers as they've come and gone.
The words they've whispered,
the secrets kept.
They've all been my spring whenever
old man winter would pound
at my door.

At the right moment,
all lovers are the right person–
Stepping forward to cross my path
each has started a funny feeling...
Each has been a celebration of love.

Holding my heart suspended in time,
the passion raging inside me.
A warmth close enough to touch.
Forever building love's memory bank.

DEAR DARLING

I thought of you today.
Your memory keeps walking through my head.
And as I look back into the mirror of love,
I remember the passion
From your heart to mine.

You will always be
The smile that crosses
My face during the day
That I want to take with me wherever I go.

Yet I want to wake up with you tomorrow
On satin sheets lost in your bedroom eyes,
And know that our heart-shaped love
Is never out of season.

INDIVIDUALITY

I will capture your heart
And never once
Will I break it.

I want a love
That will burn
As bright as candles.

I want you
As you should be
(Had we never met)
And the way
You truly are
Is exactly the way
You should stay.

SHOW MERCY

Walk gently through the path of my heart
For here you will find memories of love
And some may even bear your name
If you should strike a familiar cord
Do not hesitate to understand
The heart is the last to forget
And the last to let go.

SUNDAY IN BED

Staying in bed
making love for hours
the swaying curtain
from an open window
almost noon
lusty sexy remnants
of our sensuous pleasures
in a king-size brass
unwinding
Sunday in the suburbs
where we now live
in the town home neighborhood
of middle-class life
fathers wash their car on driveways
while pre-school children laugh and
ride tricycles down manicured blocks
Garage sales: bikes and baby clothes
to buy and in the close distance
the smell of charcoal until dusk
We listen to the radio in the stillness
of the day from behind wrinkled sheets
the sun smiles down and the Sunday
paper is on the foot of the bed

LOVE'S CHRONOSCOPE

In all the eternities
that we share today,
still cling to me
with all your tomorrows:
for there is nothing
that the heart
can't understand,
nothing that love
can't fix,
and nothing that time
can't heal.

YOUR LOVE TIPTOES QUIETLY

I can't recall being in love with you
any time before that day,
I knew that my heart was being
carried on a rainbow
sometimes orange or yellow
sometimes red or green.

My heart was the mark
and Cupid's arrow was straight.

Love took so many weeks
for a full moon
    to smile down
I might have left
with my faithful companion loneliness
but before too long
flames of passion
    burned in your eyes.

MAYBE

Maybe you only loved me until
It was time to love someone else.
Or maybe you loved me with a childhood naivety
Where little boys dream of being men one day.

Maybe you and I seemed like a
Good idea at the time,
Or maybe our love was something
Too little...too late...

Those I have left
can educate you
I don't return
Charity begins at home
While you made all your
Charitable contributions
out in the world,
Love went lacking on
the home front.

Now to try to rewrite
Our unfinished stanza-
My broken heart
Cannot find the words.

FAIR-WEATHER LOVER

I never met my lover on a sunny day
I always met him when the moon
Shadowed the heavens
He was magic
He was magic in the moonlight
He was the kind of guy
That could see inside my soul
He made me love him
He stole my heart
I soon realized I was searching
For a thousand tender moments

All lovers love a come-in-from-the-rain
Kind of love
It's like an anchor when
You are adrift at sea
Yet still the storm rages on
Inside my soul to this very day.

SOFT GENTLE NIGHTS

The heart holds tighter
than what it gives to infatuation.
It pulls us to a consuming blaze
on this night full of passion.

I am on fire
    all over.
I touch your hand
so that I may feel
the link from my heart to yours.

I see inside your soul
each time I am in your embrace
and lost in your bedroom eyes.

ACKNOWLEDGEMENT

Without a diary of what loves owes you
the dos and don'ts
what happens to us while loving
is welcomed with open-arms
       if not open-heart.

I loved and I was loved.
As is love's master plan,
more hearts let me in
than kept me at bay.
As memories fad and are rekindled,
the regularity of time comes
and goes in this same fashion.

The joy of a thousand tender moments
and what is left to fate
endures as the great "Oscar"
though love without "Oscar" or "Emmy"

is more than enough.

UNLOCKED DOORS

There is always another lover to love
Beyond today's lover
Always another door of passion
To open to another room.

REFLECTIONS

If I could wrap the message in your eyes
                    around me
I know I would.

There is comfort in your arms
    on cold winter nights
and something inviting and reassuring
in your smile.

It may be that love
        heartbeat to heartbeat
builds a safety net.

Our close quiet moments
        forever leave footprints on the
beaches of my mind.

FULL IS...

Full is a thread of close quiet moments
held together by a calm at the center of
the storm and a come-in-from-the-rain
kind of love.

Full is the shade of passion
when we hang out the "do not disturb"
sign and share breakfast in bed.

Full is gifts of the heart-
we have something that feels really
comfortable and wherever we are-
it is home.

DEFINITION

To find a special place
is the essence of all belonging
This is how it goes
Especially in the relationship
between lovers
As more tender moments are spent
with that special someone
The flames of passion towards
that special someone
Become more deciphered

I think of you
As a lover,
as someone with whom
I have shared
a sure and simple love
And from this opportunity
I have come to
feel towards you
As I do towards my
past meaningful others.

SO BE IT

I know I can walk off into
the sunset with you...But
I won't
Not to learn how many
spoons of sugar you take
with your coffee or
give you
the key
to my
heart

I'll always love you...
I know great love
stories are not
written this way and
If you want me to
be your wife you
can't go and marry
someone else...But you did
(So be it)
...I can only regret something
I've never done for myself...But
regret being your wife?

Not I! I've been
a wife
(All women are
sooner or later)...But

She will never be me
and...I never want to
be anything like her... That's
why you're here with me now
and not her... So
no...I won't marry you...
not to learn how many
spoons of sugar you take with
your coffee or give you the
key to my heart...You can't
be a spouse to me that
I haven't already
been to
someone
else

I know I can walk off
into the sunset with you
But I won't

OLD TOWN

Colorless clouds press
against the horizon
until night fall makes
        an entrance.

In a split second
daylight narrows,
grows to quiet dusk
then total darkness—and stays.
And yet old lovers
still walk these cobblestone
        streets.

Whatever intrigue has made them linger,
I watch from afar with heavy heart.
If I should walk these cobblestone
streets at midnight,
would I too find true love?

HEARTBURN

Why is it there are no
All night drug stores
I can go to when my senses
Have had too much of
Your sweet indulgences?

Why are there
No quick fizzle fiz
Tablets to take
When my heart is
Heavy in my chest?

Medical science
hasn't come
that far
after all!

TRUE LOVE COMES

True love comes as the break of dawn to each day,
certainly as the moon, as she sings the song of night,
like the rainbow after the storm,
she comes with magic,
she comes forth-
silently.

True love appears as the mountains stand united towards
heaven, certainly it comes as the heart dares beat,
like the flower that must grow from sun,
not lingering behind in shadows,
not rushing hastily forth,
but at the right moment-
patiently.

True love arrives as snow comes with winter,
certainly as candles glow,
as birds sing of spring,
then it lingers-
eternally.

LOVE'S MIRROR

The heart in some kind of abyss
        while I was lonely,
it waited.

The only way to understand love
is to reach out and touch another.
I would not miss
sleeping alone or dinner for one,
empty arms in the night
that loneliness gives way to.

Where else but in love
do we meet our true selves?

MIDNIGHT INTERLUDE

I made
   the night caps
Thus letting another adventure
      unravel our souls.
Your ever-calling eyes now
beg me to come to far-away places.
We are brought closer by the
magic of the night.

Passion takes her place.
The stage is set.
Each of us has suddenly gone
beyond formal hand shakes
and small talk.

BETTER HALF

I am touched by you often
touched by your bright beautiful smiles
and the private corridors
down the halls
of your mind

I am touched by a special part of you
that touches me even when
you are not here

I can be myself
no name-dropping
no unhappy endings
so I surrender
playful and uplifted
when your whisper is penetrating
juicy mouth-watering love.

ANIMAL MAGNETISM

I know love
by its private number.

I am thrilled
of what is yet to come
or what you will bring
and all that is in store
when loving you
I return often
for the magic.

So for just this once
please hold back
the dawn
for seductive and precious
is midnight.

RECKLESS HEART

I believe most lovers
      are loved
for what they bring to a relationship,
not for what they perceive it to be.
It only takes a pair of passing eyes
to give a heart the chance to dream.

Good-bye is love's lost wilderness.
The lover inside me still hears
only an echo recalling
from the sounds of past lovers.
Good-bye still tears away at the
      core of my soul.
And having back the gold and
silver of ten summers ago,
I would be there riding off
into the sunset
      eager for the next lover-
giving my heart away even before
knowing a heart would
be mind in return.

REFLECTIONS

I discover you walking the beaches of my mind
leaving your footprints forever there
in layers of memories
I wait

in an instant

your voice

or after-shave lotion

or sun glasses

blown up

larger than life

like some neon billboard

and yet

where are you now?

old habits die hard

this haunting melody

at the core of my being

engulfing me

and yet you will always be

the beating part of my heart

CLOSE QUIET MOMENTS

Our hearts should be inextricably
bound even for just this one night
we will feel found not lost
until all our wounds have healed
mouthfuls and hand fulls
      of love
through the soft darkness,
deep into each others' bedroom eyes
and the private corridors
      of each others' mind.

EVEN ETERNITY IS MEASURABLE

I am animal magnetism
Conceived in the soul of passion
And defined in the hearts
Of lovers I have known

Within myself I am love forever true
Yet I am days of future passed
As the lovers who have shared
My bed will attest

I can regulate my emotions
But I can't regulate theirs
So in essence, I must hold on to
The memory of love's valuable
Lesson and let others feel what
I feel and remember what I
Remember even for just
A brief moment

I SAW YOU TODAY

I saw you today
...you were with her
I could have gotten closer
But why?
...That my heart would
skip a beat?
...That my skin would
break out into a cold sweat?

I stared
(a secret voyeur)
from across the way
You had your face
tucked down into some book
(always the intellect)
My soul for a brief moment
danced again and

It wasn't until the two
of you walked out of the
bookstore that I remembered
how I thought in high school
you had hung the moon...My
early poems were all about you...
Oh, sweet perfection

You hailed a taxi
smiling
probably on your way to our
restaurant to be at our favorite
table with her...I stood there
feeling almost like a Peeping
Tom, my abandon heart has
seen better days

CELEBRATION

I thank you Darling for lots this incredible time:
for a come-in-from-rain kind of love
and an April rose in December snow; and for all
that is between your heart and mine

(I who have had my heart broken am loved again today,
and this is the calm at the center of the storm;
this is the sunshine of your love gleaming through:
and a special coming together)

How could I in the warmth of your eyes
when you took my hand
and reached out and touched the smile
forming on my face-ever doubt you?

(Now I listen to the silence-for in it
your heart speaks and
the melody of your unspoken love
teaches my heart to sing)

LOVE'S RETURN

My broken heart has mended
And now I am staying
I have found my way back home
To a lover who took me in with open arms

When you truly love someone
You should love them forever
I knew I had to make peace within
Before I could make peace with you

Good-bye was my cartoon
Filled with characters from
Some make-believe movie
The more the pain grew—
The more I pushed you away

My broken heart has mended
And now I am staying
I have found my way back home
To a lover who took me in
With open arms

HAUNTING

Haunting your heart
listening to each sigh
I will recall always
in microscopic details
of an all-absorbing love affair
as I beat on and on
within-back and forth
I am stretched over
rows of souvenirs
and I am absorbed
by rhythmic patterns of yesterday
I see love lines
like laser beams in space
along rare and beautiful moments
you and I
forbidden fruit in an unfinished play
to disconnect my heart
from yours
to live without you now
or die trying
however the timeless rhythm of love
left us.

LASTING IMPRESSIONS

It's always the lovers that do the most damage
The ones you know so well.
        Held in motel rooms
                        one-night-stands
and forgotten.

Sometimes I think we were meant to be lovers.
To get to know one another,
to get close enough to hear each others'
heart beat.

But then,
someone always leaves
and it becomes the same old story.

Still, as time goes on
it is easier to remember
the motel room where we were
                than your name.

TO YOU

To you I give a consuming passion
so that you may find your way to my heart

To you I give a thousand tender moments
cause loneliness can cut like a knife

To you I give love's timeless rhythm
since every slice of destiny is just
another piece of the puzzle unraveling

SATIN SHEETS AND YOU

I look with favor
And find the fire in my eyes
Reflected back to me

I touch you
And find my heart
Has room for only one

I discover the real sense
Of the word passion
That some use so free

Today I discover that special
Lover with whom I can share
A-come-in-from-the-rain
Kind of love

Living with only myself
And all my yesterdays
Has prepared me to partake
Of this moment in time.

SWEET COMMUNION

I want to sit at the table of love.
I want to kneel at the altar
of your heart.
Darling, I adore only you.
Only you can have my treasures
upon this Earth.

ABANDON HEARTS 101

I saw you staring at the rain, my Darling
Your thoughts so far away.
Why can't things stay the same forever?
Take an example from one lover to another
We were a brief shining moment.

I can see a part of your heart will never mend
Yet another place, another time.
Everyone has cheap thrills and expensive regrets.
We are not etched in stone.

Checking out time is 2p.m.
Darling, I know it cuts like a knife.
Welcome to abandon hearts 101—
Between animal magnetism and artificial flowers
Welcome to abandon hearts 101—
Between satin sheets and midnight lullabies.
Once you understand love gives us all a second chance,
You will do just fine here in abandon hearts 101

NIGHT RHYTHMS

Moist softness
of our lips
moonlight dancing
on our skin
the music
in our souls
I want to go
the distance
with you tonight.

I WANT TO GIVE YOU

I want to give you
forever the song of Love

I want to give you
(taken from a December snow)
an April rose
and the sounds of the night
that only lovers hear

I want to take you deeper
into love than you have
ever been before,
all this I want to give you

INTOXICATION

Last night making love with you
Was like drinking fine vintage wine.
With each sip,
My senses were heightened.
You caressed my heart and
Made it feel like
My body feels when lying in the nude
Between satin sheets.
Your unique taste had been acquired
Within the vineyard of other bodies.
All too soon morning did come.
Your good-bye left
me with a hang-over
And the taste of love
upon my tongue.

SOMEWHERE IN MY LONG AGO

I am the priestess who tends
the sacred fires
on the altar
of the temple of Love.

Slowly I move through time and space.
The indelible feelings on my heart.
I look around this old world,
a celestial sphere of watercolors

And I see us
as timeless and delicate moments,
love letters,
a yellow rose,
stored away in love's time capsule.

FOR THIS ONE NIGHT

Grasp on to my heart
as no one ever has
while we keep
this love alive.

I beg that you
remain long enough
to help me understand
love's valuable lesson.

FOUND

You came into my life today.
Yesterday I heard your voice
whispering softly as you called,
an echo in the back of my mind.

I found you in the river of time.
Other lovers upon my heart knocked,
fleeing, I escaped them all.

A large burst of sun,
you gleam bright before my eyes.
now– I my cup overflowing and with you,
stand ready to face the unknown.

OUR LOVE WILL KEEP

We endure. Many years.
I mentally record experiences
that have been a part
    of our love.

There is a time for gifts of the heart
so I look inside your soul
and see love you can slip
into like a pair of
    old slippers
comfortable. a perfect fit.

A SILVER LINING SOMETIMES THERE

It is not easy living only with souvenirs
Only time can soothe the pain
And the clouds of love are great in number
Especially the ones that bring rain
But the past is gone and her souvenirs
Sit on the mantle looking out of place
So I'll take the rain
And give your heart enough breathing space.

The sky of love is cloudy
And the darkest hour is just before daylight
But a hug or kiss
Is like a silver lining shining bright
And when you whisper I am yours it eases
The pain in my heart
Cause you are here with me at this time
And for now you and her are apart.

I can live with the clouds of love is there's
A silver lining sometimes there
I can carry the the burden for awhile
Although my heart is well aware
You will be dreaming of her
When we're holding each other tight—
I will not despair
I can live with the clouds of love if there's
A silver lining sometimes there.

ASPEN STATE OF MIND

This is one of those evenings.
Unrehearsed.
Light falling snow.
Magical dreamy December.

I am weak in the knees.
I search your eyes for
The colors of sunset.

My heart is home—
You are the fireplace
Where at the end of the day,
I come to warm my dreams.

PATIENCE

I have been always in search
Of my meaningful other self
Most all of my days.

I could have waited until
The day after eternity
Because I was waiting for you.
You were worth the wait.

YOU STILL...

You still carry that photo
of me in your wallet.
You still can savor the moment.
My mind's eye holds beautiful pictures.
...I will always be
the first girl who gave you flowers.

You still know my weak spot.
You still will be here
even after eternity takes you.
...I will be your girl
forever.

PURPLE HEARTS

We are veterans:
Our hearts have been
on the front line.
I'd like to think
you and I have
been on the same side
in this bloody war.
Funny how there are no
medals for good-bye.

LOVE: THE GREAT TEACHER

Love that rejuvenates the walls of this body,
That made the adolescence and softened this hard frame,
Taught us to experience the power of love,
To listen to the silence-for in it the heart speaks,
To put aside cheap thrills and expensive regrets,
Brings us new April mornings:
Such celebration is ours, if this is our moment,
We fear no more of our hearts being abandoned,
Or even the thought of turning back time,
The fury of desire, the animal magnetism:
Love, doing this to us, may let us see
Forever in each other's eyes.

BIBLE IN HIS HAND

His church is like heaven sitting up on a high hill,
With a stained glass window
That reads: "Come all that will".
Though he seems like any other preacher
With a heart that is so kind,
He's standing there with the bible in his hand,
And cheating on his mind.

Through the week he comes to visit me,
At church on Sunday he kneels down to pray.
Dear heavenly Father won't you wash my sins away?
With his eyes closed you would swear he had a direct line-
As he kneels there with the bible in his hand,
And cheating on his mind.

You should see him lead the choir.
Sometimes he even testifies.
Still what he feels for me,
You know the preacher can't deny.
With his love he can soothe my troubled heart,
Yet lost souls for the Lord he can find
As he stands there with the bible in his hand,
And cheating on his mind.

CONTENTMENT

Oh, what a bright city is Eternity,
Stirs your soul, and makes you breathless.
My cherished love; and all you are,
You are someone to belong to, even more.
Those bright portals loved of many
Would glisten as if shooting stars.

Stirs you even more, Eternity's open gate,
And upward in grand style comes
From your warm heart your welcome sigh.
Still inside your arms is my favorite place.

But you are the satin pillow my heart sleeps upon:
You are here all streets into Ecstasy.
Uplifted I am made whole, and forever
At home a satisfied lover.

EXAMINATION

Love, like a nylon stocking,
is made up of many threads
which interwoven form a pattern.
To detach but one
and examine it alone,
not only takes away
from the totality
but gives the thread worthlessness.

EXITS

Good-bye is never a clean break.
There is always the memory.
The after-taste.
It lingers.
Leaving so slowly.
Cutting like a knife all the while.
I have to leave you now.
I know in time one day
My heart will follow.
Eternity is never as long as
A broken heart takes to mend.